Drawn from the Well

by Salema Cornick
illustrated by Sonya Vine

A collection of illustrated bible verses
to encourage, guide, comfort and empower.

First edition, published in the United Kingdom by Onwards and Upwards Publishers (2020). ISBN: 978-1-78815-519-9.

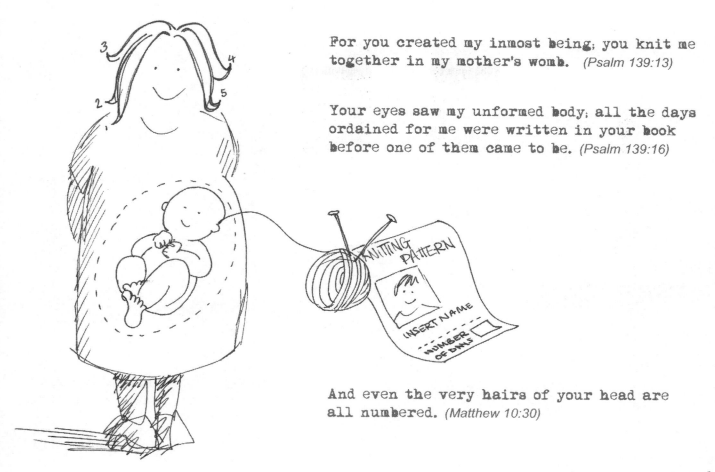

For you created my inmost being; you knit me together in my mother's womb. *(Psalm 139:13)*

Your eyes saw my unformed body; all the days ordained for me were written in your book before one of them came to be. *(Psalm 139:16)*

And even the very hairs of your head are all numbered. *(Matthew 10:30)*

3

Do not be afraid, little flock, for your father has been pleased to give you the Kingdom. *(Luke 12:32)*

4

I give them eternal life, and they shall never perish;
no one will snatch them out of my hand. *(John 10:28)*

Call to me and I will answer you... *(Jeremiah 33:3)*

But the fruit of the spirit is love, joy, peace, patience, kindness, goodness, faithfulness, gentleness, self-control. *(Galatians 5:22-23)*

The axe is already at the root of the trees; and every tree that does not produce good fruit will be cut down and thrown into the fire. *(Matthew 3:10)*

The light shines in the darkness, and the darkness has not overcome it. *(John 1:5)*

In the same way, let your light shine before others, that they may see your good deeds and glorify your Father in heaven. *(Matthew 5:16)*

Your word is a lamp for my feet,
a light on my path. *(Psalm 119:105)*

Be angry and do not sin; do not let the sun go down on your anger. *(Ephesians 4:26)*

Get rid of all bitterness, rage and anger, brawling and slander,
along with every form of malice. *(Ephesians 4:31)*

Put on the full armour of God, so that you will be able to stand firm against the schemes of the devil. *(Ephesians 6:11)*

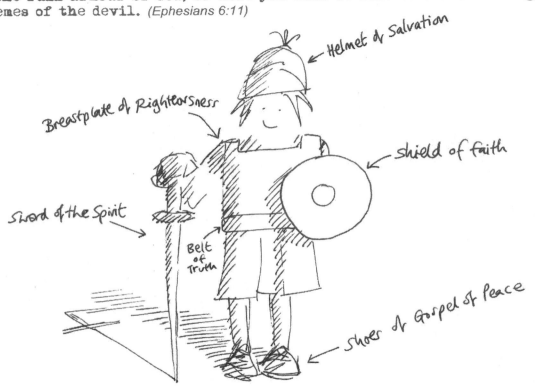

Helmet of Salvation

Breastplate of Righteousness

shield of faith

Sword of the Spirit

Belt of Truth

shoes of Gospel of Peace

For though we walk in the flesh, we do not war according to the flesh, for the weapons of our warfare are not of the flesh, but divinely powerful for the destruction of fortresses. *(2 Corinthians 10:3-4)*

Like a fluttering sparrow or a darting swallow,
an undeserved curse does not come to rest.
(Proverbs 26:2)

Bless those who curse you, pray for those who
mistreat you. *(Luke 6:28)*

Above all, love each other deeply,
because love covers over a multitude of sins. *(1 Peter 4:8)*

Hatred stirs up conflict, but love covers over all wrongs. *(Proverbs 10:12)*

And over all these virtues put on love, which binds them all together in perfect unity. *(Colossians 3:14)*

Let love and faithfulness never leave you;
bind them around your neck,
write them on the tablet of your heart.
(Proverbs 3:3)

The Lord does not look at the things people look at. People look at the outward appearance, but the Lord looks at the heart. *(1 Samuel 16:7)*

Perfume and incense bring joy to the heart, and the pleasantness of a friend springs from their heartfelt advice. *(Proverbs 27:9)*

But thanks be to God, who always leads us as captives in Christ's triumphal procession and uses us to spread the aroma of the knowledge of him everywhere. *(2 Corinthians 2:14)*

Then Jesus declared, "I am the bread of life. Whoever comes to me will never go hungry, and whoever believes in me will never be thirsty. *(John 6:35)*

Come, all you who are thirsty, come to the waters; and you who have no money, come, buy and eat! Come, buy wine and milk without money and without cost. *(Isaiah 55:1)*

In the same way, I tell you, there is rejoicing in the presence of the angels of God over one sinner who repents. *(Luke 15:10)*

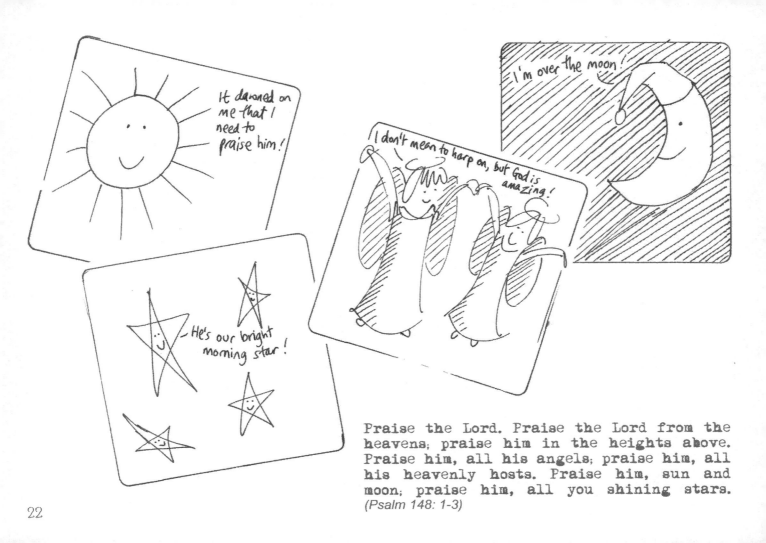

Praise the Lord. Praise the Lord from the heavens; praise him in the heights above. Praise him, all his angels; praise him, all his heavenly hosts. Praise him, sun and moon; praise him, all you shining stars.
(Psalm 148: 1-3)

Praise the Lord from the earth, you great sea creatures and all ocean depths, lightning and hail, snow and clouds, stormy winds that do his bidding, you mountains and all hills, fruit trees and all cedars, wild animals and all cattle, small creatures and flying birds, kings of the earth and all nations, you princes and all rulers on earth, young men and women, old men and children. Let them praise the name of the Lord, for his name alone is exalted; his splendour is above the earth and the heavens.
(Psalm 148:7-13)

Because you are my help,
I sing in the shadow of your wings
(Psalm 63:7)

Give thanks in all circumstances;
for this is God's will for you in Christ Jesus.
(1 Thessalonians 5:18)

Be joyful in hope,
patient in affliction,
faithful in prayer.
(Romans 12:12)

The name of the Lord is a strong tower;
The righteous runs into it and is safe.
(Proverbs 18:10)

The Lord is good, a refuge in times of trouble. He cares for those who trust in him.
(Nahum 1:7)

Listen! Listen to the roar of his voice, to the rumbling that comes from his mouth. He unleashes his lightning beneath the whole heaven and sends it to the ends of the earth. After that comes the sound of his roar; He thunders with his majestic voice. When his voice resounds, he holds nothing back. God's voice thunders in marvellous ways; He does great things beyond our understanding.
(Job 37 2-5)

The lion has roared - who will not fear? The Sovereign Lord has spoken - who can but prophesy?
(Amos 3:8)

27

For we are God's handiwork, created in Christ Jesus to do good works,
which God prepared in advance for us to do. *(Ephesians 2:10)*

Yet you, Lord, are our Father. We are the clay, you are the potter;
we are all the work of your hand. *(Isaiah 64:8)*

But who are you, a human being, to talk back to God? "Shall what is formed say to the one who formed it, 'Why did you make me like this?'" Does not the potter have the right to make out of the same lump of clay some pottery for special purposes and some for common use?   *(Romans 9:20-21)*

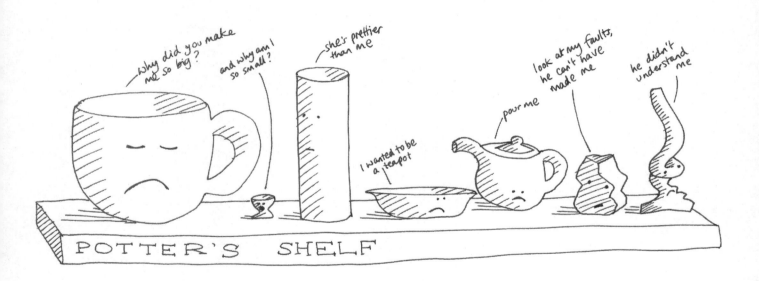

As iron sharpens iron, so one person sharpens another. *(Proverbs 27:17)*

Therefore encourage one another and build each other up. *(1 Thessalonians 5:11)*

For I was hungry and you gave me something to eat, I was thirsty and you gave me something to drink, I was a stranger and you invited me in, I needed clothes and you clothed me, I was sick and you looked after me, I was in prison and you came to visit me.' *(Matthew 25:35-36)*

Ask and it will be given to you;
seek and you will find;
knock and the door will be opened to you.
(Matthew 7:7)

If I had cherished sin in my heart,
the Lord would not have listened.
(Psalm 66:18)

Then you will know the truth
and the truth will set you free.
(John 8:32)

For this is what the Sovereign Lord says: I myself will search for my sheep and look after them. *(Ezekiel 34:11)*

For the Son of Man came to seek and to save that which was lost. *(Luke 19:10)*

Those who sow with tears will reap with songs of joy. *(Psalm 126:5)*

Hear my prayer, Lord, listen to my cry for help; do not be deaf to my weeping. *(Psalm 39:12)*

My friends scorn me; My eyes pour out tears to God. *(Job 16:20)*

The Lord is close to the **brokenhearted** and saves those who are crushed in spirit.
(Psalm 34:18)

He **heals** the **brokenhearted**
and **binds** up their wounds.
(Psalm 147:3)

Have I not commanded you? Be strong and courageous. Do not be afraid; do not be discouraged, for the Lord your God will be with you wherever you go. *(Joshua 1:9)*

You rule over the surging sea; when its waves mount up, you still them. *(Psalm 89:9)*

We have this hope as an anchor for the soul, firm and secure. *(Hebrews 6:19)*

Then they cried out to the Lord in their trouble, and he brought them out of their distress. He stilled the storm to a whisper; the waves of the sea were hushed. *(Psalm 107:28-29)*

When you pass through the waters, I will be with you; and when you pass through the rivers, they will not sweep over you. When you walk through the fire, you will not be burned; the flames will not set you ablaze. *(Isaiah 43:2)*

Even though I walk through the valley of the shadow of death, I will fear no evil, for you are with me; your rod and your staff, they comfort me. *(Psalm 23:4)*

Seek first his kingdom and his righteousness, and all these things will be given to you as well. *(Matthew 6:33)*

Seek good, not evil, that you may live. Then the Lord God Almighty will be with you, just as you say he is. *(Amos 5:14)*

The people living in darkness have seen a great light; on those living in the land of the shadow of death a light has dawned. *(Matthew 4:16)*

Let the fields be jubilant, and everything in them; let all the trees of the forest sing for joy. *(Psalm 96:12)*

For you shall go out with joy, And be led out with peace; The mountains and the hills shall break forth into singing before you, And all the trees of the field shall clap their hands. *(Isaiah 55:12)*

Carry each other's burdens, and in this way you
will fulfil the law of Christ. *(Galatians 6:2)*

We who are strong ought to bear with
the failings of the weak and not to
please ourselves. *(Romans 15:1)*

Trust in the Lord with all your heart and lean not on your own understanding.
(Proverbs 3:5)

Therefore, since we are surrounded by such a great cloud of witnesses, let us throw off everything that hinders and the sin that so easily entangles, and let us run with perseverance the race marked out for us. *(Hebrews 12:1)*

Wine is a mocker and beer a brawler; whoever is led astray by them is not wise.
(Proverbs 20:1)

Cast but a glance at riches, and they are gone, for they will surely sprout wings and fly off to the sky like an eagle. *(Proverbs 23:5)*

Those who trust in their riches will fall, but the righteous will thrive like a green leaf. *(Proverbs 11:28)*

What good is it for someone to gain the whole world, yet forfeit their soul? *(Mark 8:36)*

Set your minds on things above, not on earthly things. *(Colossians 3:2)*

Pleasant words are a honeycomb, sweet to the soul and healing to the bones.
(Proverbs 16:24)

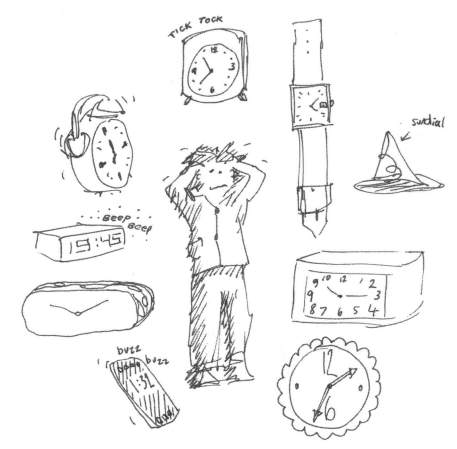

Can any one of you by worrying add a single hour to your life? *(Matthew 6:27)*

Praise be to the Lord, to God our Saviour, who daily bears our burdens. *(Psalm 68:19)*

Cast all your anxiety on him because he cares for you. *(1 Peter 5:7)*

But now ask the beasts, and let them teach you;
And the birds of the heavens, and let them tell you.
Or speak to the earth, and let it teach you;
And let the fish of the sea declare to you.
Who among all these does not know
That the hand of the Lord has done this,
In whose hand is the life of every living thing,
And the breath of all mankind? *(Job 12:7-10)*

Both riches and honour come from you, and you rule over all, and in your hand is power and might; and it lies in your hand to make great and to strengthen everyone. *(1 Chronicles 29:12)*

Let the morning bring me word of your unfailing love, for I have put my trust in you. Show me the way I should go, for to you I entrust my life. *(Psalm 143:8)*

The steadfast love of the Lord never ceases; his mercies never come to an end; they are new every morning; great is your faithfulness. *(Lamentations 3:22-23)*

On my bed I remember you; I think of you through the watches of the night. *(Psalm 63:6)*

"I am the light of the world. Whoever follows me will never walk in darkness, but will have the light of life." *(John 8:12)*

58

How abundant are the good things that you have stored up for those who fear you, that you bestow in the sight of all, on those who take refuge in you. *(Psalm 31:19)*

He stores up sound wisdom for the upright. *(Proverbs 2:7)*

Is not this laid up in store with me, sealed up in my treasuries? *(Deuteronomy 32:34)*

Hide me from the conspiracy of the wicked, from the plots of evildoers. *(Psalm 64:2)*

I am in the midst of lions; I am forced to dwell among ravenous beasts - men whose teeth are spears and arrows, whose tongues are sharp swords. *(Psalm 57:4)*

But I trust in your unfailing love; my heart rejoices in your salvation. *(Psalm 13:5)*

Submit yourselves, then, to God. Resist the devil, and he will flee from you. *(James 4:7)*

Be alert and of sober mind. Your enemy the devil prowls around like a roaring lion looking for someone to devour. Resist him, standing firm in the faith, because you know that the family of believers throughout the world is undergoing the same kind of sufferings. *(1 Peter 5:8-9)*

The Lord your God who goes before you will himself fight for you. *(Deuteronomy 1:30)*

For the Lord your God is the one who goes with you to fight for you against your enemies to give you victory. *(Deuteronomy 20:4)*

Jesus looked at them and said,
"With man this is impossible, but with God all things are possible." *(Matthew 19:26)*

"I am the Lord, the God of all mankind.
Is anything too hard for me?" *(Jeremiah 32:27)*

Truly I tell you, if anyone says to this mountain, 'Go, throw yourself into the sea,' and does not doubt in their heart but believes that what they say will happen, it will be done for them. *(Mark 11:23)*

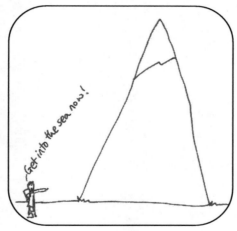

65

Instead of your shame you will receive a double portion, and instead of disgrace you will rejoice in your inheritance. And so you will inherit a double portion in your land, and everlasting joy will be yours. *(Isaiah 61:7)*

For God so loved the world
that he gave his one and only Son,
that whoever believes in him
shall not perish but have eternal life.
(John 3:16)

Therefore we do not lose heart. Though outwardly we are wasting away, yet inwardly we are being renewed day by day. *(2 Corinthians 4:16)*

And behold, I am with you always, to the end of the age. *(Matthew 28:20)*